In Gratitude

Teresa Lanowich

ISBN-13: 9781544213453

To Our Lady
my life, my sweetness, and my hope

CONTENTS

PREFACE

In 1998, I experienced profound healing from my choice of abortion. My healing came through an outpouring of extraordinary graces and the assistance of many priests. During that time, my spiritual director encouraged me to write down all the events that transpired which led me to total restoration in Christ. I did as he requested. Even though I recorded all the events about this story, I do not readily share it with others. It is so deeply personal. Many years ago, I decided to keep it private and leave it between me and God, unless he had another intention for it.

So how did my story come to you? What changed my mind? It happened in the summer of 2011 while praying my usual morning prayer form, Lectio Divina. I was meditating on a passage in scripture about the healing of the leper from the gospel of Luke:

"Now there was a man full of leprosy in one of the towns where he was; and when he saw Jesus, he fell prostrate, pleaded with him, and said, "Lord if you wish you can make me clean." Jesus stretched out his hand, touched him, and said, "I do will it. Be made clean." And the leprosy left him immediately. Then he ordered him not to tell anyone, but "Go show yourself to the priest and offer your cleansing what Moses prescribed; that will be proof for them." Luke 5:12-14

I had read this scripture passage many times over the years. However, this time was different. My heart felt pierced by the words of Luke's gospel as soon as I read them. While mediating, these thoughts began to rise up within me: "I was the leper and you, Jesus, stretched out your hand and healed me of my sins of abortion. You restored my soul to beauty and dignity." Then, in an incredible moment of grace, the words, "Go show yourself to the priest....that will be proof for them," resounded in my heart. I instantly knew with an inexplicable certitude that my story of healing from the sins of abortion was meant for priests.

As my healing did not come by the usual way - rather through extraordinary movements of the Holy Spirit, I do feel reticence to talk about it. However, I know God is asking me to share this healing story of his great mercy and love with his priests. Even though I do not know his intention for you, I do know God's intention for me - to make myself visible and transparent to you. I think of Saint Paul's letter to the Corinthians when he wrote, "To each individual the manifestation of the Spirit is given for some benefit." For me, the benefits have been deeper faith, greater hope, and an expansion of my heart for greater love. However, only you will determine the benefit that this story has for you.

The consequences of my choice of abortion caused deep suffering and wounding to my soul. My greatest challenge was to face this type of suffering. Once I was able to pour out my suffering and wounds to God, I became open to responding to his grace. He would draw me deeper and deeper into his inexhaustible mystery of love and mercy. I journeyed through 6 stages of healing which were assisted by Our Lady, various priests, and one seminarian. These stages were going to confession, learning the importance of the accompaniment of the Blessed Mother, making a general confession, following the shepherd, discovering the importance of names to God, and experiencing the healing power of the Eucharist. I will share with you the events that led to each stage and the insights I received from the Lord through them. All the events you are about to read are true, but the names of the priests have been changed to ensure their privacy.

As I share my witness of healing, I hope you will not be distracted by my prayer experiences. The spiritual consolations and favors I was granted were pure gift. Rather, I encourage you to look at the message of these experiences. I pray that you will be open to receive through grace what the Lord intended for you. There is an intention he desires for you to receive or he would not have invited me to share this story with his priests.

Now it is my great privilege to share my witness of what Divine Love can do to a life.

This is for you...

SACRAMENT OF RECONCILIATION

"My guilt towers higher than my head; it is a weight too heavy to bear"

Psalm 38

My first step toward healing, although not deliberate, would be an attempt at participating in the sacrament of reconciliation. It was not my abortions that brought me to confession, rather my desire to enter back fully into the church. However, the grace of this sacrament would start me on the road toward contrition over this grievous sin.

The events on the road to Reconciliation:

It was in 1988 when I had returned to my Catholic faith after leaving it for eighteen years. I decided to participate in the sacrament of reconciliation which forced me to recall my abortions. I remember that day clearly. I was terrified because I knew I had many grievous sins to confess. During those eighteen years, I had broken every commandment. Yet, it was the abortions that I felt particularly ashamed of and embarrassed to reveal. Unsteady because my legs were shaking, I leaned against the wall by the confessional as I waited on the long line. Trying to control the waves of nausea I felt, I took deep breathes. When it was my turn, I forced my body to move and walked into the confessional.

As I knelt in front of the screen, I told the priest that it was eighteen years since my last confession. He replied, "What took you so long?" I said, "I thought I could just tell God my sins and that was sufficient." He responded in a tone that I interpreted as a reprimand for my stupidity, "Why would you think that?" I tried to explain my thinking but was met with his silence. I did my best to continue my confession and said some of my sins, but I could not reveal to him that I had aborted two children. When I left the confessional, I was shaken by this encounter and felt convicted by the fact that I had withheld this serious sin.

The shame that I felt because of my choice of abortion was so great that it was necessary for me to feel some emotional safety to reveal it. The initial response of this priest did not provide that security. Now experiencing even more the gravity of this sin, I decided that I needed to find another confessor as quickly as possible. A few days later, I called Father Raymond, a priest from a local parish, to make an appointment for confession. The good Lord knew that Father Raymond was the priest who should hear this sin of abortion from me. His first response to me when he opened the door was a big smile with a warm greeting. He engaged me in casual conversation as we walked into his office. I felt very nervous, especially now that my confession would be face to face. I'm sure it was obvious to Father Raymond through my demeanor how fear ridden I was. He met my fear with great sensitivity.

While I confessed my sin of abortion to Father Raymond, he listened with a tender expression on his face. He smiled, which seemed unusual to me after revealing such an awful sin. It was as though he was happy for me that I confessed it and happy for him that he heard it. Then his response made sense to me. He gently explained the seriousness of this sin of abortion. He told me that if I had confessed this sin at the time I aborted my children (early 1970's) only a bishop could have given him, Father Raymond, the authority to absolve me. He said now as a parish priest, he would have the great privilege to absolve me of this sin of abortion without conferring with the Bishop. I remember experiencing this feeling of dignity when he expressed that the action of absolving me as his privilege. He demonstrated a great appreciation and reverence for the authority given to him to forgive me for this grievous sin. He than told me that for my penance, I was to listen to the song, "Be Not Afraid." He said, "Play it, listen to it, and meditate on the lyrics."

I was surprised to receive such a penance: I thought that I would have to say fifty rosaries for such a horrible sin. When I listened to the lyrics of the song, "Be Not Afraid," I felt as though Our Lord was speaking to me. Through the lyrics, I was reassured that the Lord loved me, and he would give me rest if I would follow him. I was inspired with the hope that Our Lord knew I was trying to follow him, and he knew that I longed for rest.

Unfortunately, it did not take long after that confession with Father

Raymond for my shame and guilt to start haunting me again. I felt disappointed and confused as to why these feelings weren't gone; in fact, they seemed to have intensified. They were debilitating at times and would come at the most unexpected moments. For example, anytime I saw a teenage girl with a baby, I would feel this sickening shame. I would condemn myself with thoughts like, "Look at the courage she had. She found a way to keep her child." This wound of guilt oozed out of me in the form of despair. When the intensity of these feelings would surface, I would think, "This is what you deserve to feel, Teresa, for what you have done." Discouraged by my own thoughts and feelings, I decided that I would never again mention my abortions to anyone. I was convinced that if I already confessed my abortions then they should be behind me. The fact that they were not was my fault. There had to be something wrong with me! I was shackled once again by the consequence of this terrible sin.

Each time, these feelings of guilt and shame would rise up; I would deliberately push them down deep within me. However, there would be moments when the guilt was too heavy to bear. I would change my mind about telling anyone and would go into the anonymity of the sacrament of reconciliation to again confess this sin. This would go on for years.

Insights I received through Confession:

Confessing my abortions was more out of fear than sorrow. I knew I did something wrong, but I was incapable of looking truthfully at the magnitude of my sin. The reality of the action that I chose to destroy my children was too severe to reflect upon. Instead, I focused on my guilt, which encased me in fear. This limited my disposition to receive the sacramental graces that I needed. Genuine remorse would only happen when I fully accepted the truth of my offense. So my spiritual, emotional, and psychological healing would not occur for years.

I would continue to struggle with guilt and shame over this sin. It would not be until I recognized the truth of my offense that I would be able to move toward healing. In time, I would discover that it would be through the loving assistance of Our Lady that I would be able to face this sin.

ACCOMPANIMENT OF THE BLESSED MOTHER

"The decree of the Lord is trustworthy giving wisdom to the simple."
Psalm 19

The second stage of healing that I entered did not occur until seven years later. This would happen after I was introduced to a relationship with Our Lady. John Paul II said in Redemptoris Mater that Mary's "yes" to being the mother of Jesus was "the point of departure from which her whole journey toward God begins a pilgrimage from start to finish." I needed to be led by her in how to say my "yes" to enter my suffering and sorrow. That would be my point of departure from which my whole journey would begin toward Jesus to be healed from the consequences of this dreadful sin of abortion. I would need the accompaniment of Our Lady to show me the way.

The events on the road to accompaniment of Our Lady:

I really struggled for quite awhile with being open to Our Lady. It would bother me to hear preaching about her or reference about any Marian devotions. "This Catholic faith is all about Jesus - not her!" I thought. My belief was if I allowed myself to get close to Our Lady, she would take my focus away from Jesus - I would be betraying him.

Then a young seminarian named Frank came into my life. He was assigned to my parish for the summer. He would talk with me about Our Lady. Before returning to seminary, he gave me a book called True Devotion to Mary by Louis de Montfort. When I read it, I kept putting it down repeatedly saying aloud, "No! Could all this really be true?" By the time I finished the book, my heart and mind were opened to the idea of a relationship with Our Lady.

I wasn't sure what to do with this new openness or how to develop a relationship with her. I decided to say the rosary periodically. As I would recite it, I would try to imagine Our Lady praying with me before Jesus for my intentions. I slowly started to view her as a concerned mother. I was praying in a new way - all to Jesus through the Immaculate Heart of Mary.

One day while reciting the Memorare, the word, *never,* became so prominent to me. That once familiar word caused me to stop and to reflect.

Remember, O most gracious Virgin Mary, that never was it known that anyone who fled to thy protection, implored thy help, or sought thine intercession was left unaided.

I thought, "Never!" Never in all of history, in any generation, has it been known that she would leave her children unaided in their needs? Never could anyone say that they turned to her and she did not help them? This was astounding to me. No one could be found in all of history who could say that they went to Our Lady for help, and she abandoned them. That moment of grace filled my mind and heart with the greatest confidence in her. As the words of the Memorare continue, it states exactly what happened to me from that instant.

Inspired by this confidence, I fly unto thee, O Virgin of virgins, my mother; to thee do I come, before thee I stand, sinful and sorrowful. O Mother of the Word Incarnate, despise not my petitions, but in thy mercy hear and answer me.

I was so inspired by this assurance in Our Lady that no one had ever been left unaided by her that now I wanted to run to her with all my petitions knowing I could count on her. A change occurred in my prayer life. It was no longer me asking and waiting for a response from God. Now, I was learning how to listen to God and discover his will for me.

My desire for Our Lady to be involved in my life grew rapidly. She truly became the mother who I always wanted and needed. It didn't take long for me to want visual reminders of her like statues and pictures throughout my house. This made me feel safe and always in her presence. I was particularly attracted to the image of Our Lady of Sorrows. It portrayed how she suffered out of love. Little did I know that soon I would be the one suffering out of love for my children through the progression of post abortive healing. This very picture of Our Lady of Sorrows would be my reminder that she knew the suffering heart of a mother. It would not be long before she would teach me how to say "yes" to pain through grace.

It happened when I was introduced to the 30 day Ignatius Exercise written in a book called Retreat with the Lord by Father John A. Hardon, S.J. This form of the spiritual exercises could be done at home with the condition of having a priest as the spiritual guide. I was interested, so I began to look for a priest to assist me. I approached four different priests about directing me through these Ignatius exercises. All four said no. Their rejection made me begin to doubt if this retreat was for me yet I still felt desirous to experience these spiritual exercises, so I decided to pray about it. I asked God to lead me to the right priest for guidance if this retreat was his will for me.

A few days later, I was attending daily mass at my parish. Father Tim, an elderly priest, was the celebrant. I have to be honest here and tell you that I definitely was not fond of this priest. He always appeared austere and grumpy whenever I saw him. There was nothing about him that was welcoming. In fact, I would avoid him if we were in the same area. That day at mass after I received the Eucharist and returned to my pew, I knew the Lord was answering my prayer for a priest to direct me. However, I was not thrilled with his answer. I felt a nudge as I knelt there to ask Father Tim if he would direct me through these exercises. "Lord, really?" I thought. The mere idea of approaching Father intimidated me. Again I thought, "Do I really want to do this retreat after all with him directing me? Lord, surely, he cannot be the one." Nevertheless, in my heart, I knew he was the priest who I was supposed to ask. After mass, I timidly approached Father Tim about directing me through this 30 day private retreat. I was expecting him to bark a "No" at me. Yet, to my great surprise, he responded, "Yes," with no hesitation.

At our initial meeting, Father Tim was very business like and went over the format that I was to use daily during prayer. He explained how I was to proceed. I had to commit to spending at least one hour a day to prayer and the suggested meditation. He told me at that time, we would meet once a week to discuss my exercises.

I proceeded as Father Tim instructed me. I never expected that on the 4th day of my spiritual exercise, the truth about my abortions would sear my soul. That day's meditation was titled Retribution for Sin; it covered death, judgment, purgatory and hell. After I read it, I thought, "I am not ready for death!" I did not realize that retribution for my sins was necessary even after I confessed them. Once I left the confessional, I thought that was it, I was covered. I never understood that I had to do reparation in some way for these sins of my life. Frightened about this reality of sin, I immediately called out to Our Lady. I felt like a terrified child wanting to grab her mother's hand.

As usual, I began the spiritual exercise with the suggested Examination of Conscience, followed by the rosary, spontaneous prayer, and the assigned meditation of the day, which as I stated, was retribution for sin. Then, I carefully began to survey my past life situations. I examined my conscience again for any grievous offenses or acts for which I had not repented. Praying to Our Lady, I asked her to help me recall anything that needed to be exposed. I thought, "I have already confessed any mortal sins I committed, especially the abortions which I confessed numerous times over the years". So part of me felt secure that there was nothing hidden to be uncovered, but the other part of me felt worried that I had overlooked something serious. Even though I felt nervous, I was open to anything Our Lady would want me to see. I sat quietly, closed my eyes, and listened to the rhythm of my breathing.

Suddenly, something quite extraordinary happened - I fell into a dreamlike state. I was walking with a large crowd of people. They were all ages, none of whom I recognized. I saw a road winding through vast open space and the only sound was the cadence of walking feet. I felt confused and anxious as I stretched to look above the crowd. There ahead, I saw two huge golden gates. As I drew closer, my heart began to race. I saw Jesus standing at the gate with two small children in his arms. One child appeared to be five years old and the other two years old. Their deep olive complexion warmed the creamy ivory colored robes that they were wearing. Jesus was looking directly at me with eyes of love. The children were squeezing his neck tightly as they giggled. He kissed and hugged the two children and then carefully put them down. They gleefully ran away. As I arrived at the gate, the echo of their laughter greeted me. My eyes despondently looked into Jesus'- his glance was calling me in to enter through the gate.

Overcome with sorrow, my entire body weakened; I fell to my knees weeping. I realized the children he was holding were the two babies who I aborted. Those two children were the precious gifts that he sent to me that I not only rejected but also destroyed. Jesus hears my heart as I whisper, "Lord I am not worthy to enter."

I then awoke from this dreamlike state crying bitterly. What had I done! I was devastated, heartbroken at the reality of what I just saw. These were my children, my flesh and blood whom I killed. I had never really pictured them as real children. I could not allow myself to think such thoughts and live with what I had chosen to do. Now there was no denying it. I could not claim ignorance because ignorance of these crimes did not remove for me the grievousness of my act as I now saw the truth. I could not even ask for mercy, as I saw Jesus' love for me is evident through the way he looked at me. His eyes were telling me of his desire for me to enter into his kingdom.

I realized how serious my offense was and felt humbled. There was no escape from the consequence of destroying the lives of my two children, whom I now recognized as real and precious people. For the first time since my abortions, I felt true contrition for these sins. My retribution and purification had immediately begun through the heartbreaking suffering of knowing that I offended the one who loves me, Jesus. Feeling sick over this offense I called out to my most Blessed Mother, begging her to help me to bear this sorrow. I trusted her to assist me and knew that she would not have helped me see this truth if it were not good for my soul. Now, I had to trust her to help me to live with it. I desired to suffer in some way to show Our Lord my intense remorse. My suffering would come through the crushing feeling of separation from my aborted children and the lost opportunity of being their mother. I desperately wanted another chance to be their mother again. The full meaning of the fourth day meditation became crystal clear, retribution for sin, the importance of it, and the necessity for it.

The day arrived for my meeting with Father Tim. I had only spoken with him once at our initial meeting. I was frightened to reveal this visual prayer experience to him. I still perceived Father Tim as a stern and austere priest. How would he respond to me? Was he going to think that I am some kind of nut? I felt nervous to tell him face to face this shameful truth about my abortions and intimidated to share this startling experience of seeing my children with Jesus. "Take courage Teresa and tell him," I thought. "Trust that the good Lord really did know what he was doing when he chose Father Tim."

When I explained to Father Tim what I had experienced in my prayer time, his first response with a wry smile was, "I did not know that I would be working with a mystic." I was unfamiliar with the word mystic but his smile indicated to me that it was not a bad thing. That was the most emotion I saw from him the whole time we met during my 33 days of the Ignatius Exercise. He continued with his reliable calm demeanor to reassure me that my experience was not totally unusual, especially during this type of spiritual exercise. Father then talked to me about purgatory and how this prayer occurrence that I had was in a sense a glimpse of that. He told me that upon death, we will see the full truth of all our sins. Then, Father Tim said that it was a blessing for me to see only one of my sins and not all of them together at once.

I told Father that I had confessed my sins of abortion but had not felt this level of sorrow. He reassured me that it was good to feel that level of sorrow and not to be afraid of this reparation, for it is necessary. Father Tim then encouraged me to say the morning offering everyday to help prepare my soul for death. He went into detail about the meaning of the words of this prayer, so I could feel confident in the benefits of reciting it. This brought me comfort to know that I could do reparation for my sins daily by beginning my day with the morning offering - a practice that I have been faithful to since. He also told me to call him before our weekly appointment if I needed to talk to him, especially after hearing about such an experience.

Insights I received through accompaniment of Our Lady:

I learned that a vital part of this post abortive healing journey was to turn to Our Lady. She is my mother who understands the depths of sorrow. This relationship with Our Lady was a treasure God gave me. In his mercy, he bestowed upon me as the scripture says, "wisdom to the simple" by showing me how quickly I can come before him with her assistance. In a moment's time, I understood the profound truth of what I had done. It was shown to me in such a loving way.

I am convinced that upon my request for her help, I received an abundance of grace. Through her assistance, I was able to enter into the depth of sorrow that I needed to experience. It was she who personally accompanied me to her son, Jesus. He, who with no words, told me he forgives me, loves me, and wants me with him for all eternity.

I also understood that part of Our Lord's mercy was illuminating the truth about the sin that I committed. I needed to enter into the pain of this truth to make room for him to heal me. This was a necessary reparation. To live with such a truth would be extremely painful and a daily challenge as I continued on the path to healing. After experiencing such an intense prayer experience, I felt certitude that it was necessary for me to continue this journey with the accompaniment of Our Lady. Part of her guidance would be to lead me to her son through her beloved priests.

GENERAL CONFESSION

"Strengthen the hands that are feeble, make firm the knees that are weak, say to those whose hearts are frightened. Be strong fear not here is your God...He comes to save you."

Isaiah 35

This third phase of healing emerged more rapidly due to the depth of sorrow that I was feeling. The genuine remorse over my personal responsibility for the grave action of abortion was one thing; now, having to live with that truth was a whole new reality. I struggled with how to accept and to exist with this realization of aborting real children, my children.

The events on the road to General Confession:

Trying to get a handle on my sorrow, I began to rationalize my decisions to abort. I would tell myself, "You were too young, scared, and ignorant to know what you were doing. You didn't really understand at the time that you were destroying a human life." I tried to soothe myself with these thoughts. Then, unexpectedly, while sitting at a red traffic light one afternoon waiting for it to turn green, my eyes filled with tears as grief stabbed my heart with the mental image of my children at the gate with Jesus. I could not escape this truth that our Lady helped me to see. Another time, while shopping for dinner in the grocery store, I saw at the end of the aisle, an olive complexion five- year- old girl sitting in a shopping cart pushed by her young teenage mother. Immediately, I was reminded of my aborted child. I felt my body tremble while an incredible sick feeling consumed me. I tried to compose myself, but the sadness was more than I could bear, and it took all that I had not to collapse right there on the floor in tears. I could not escape this daily sorrow. At any given moment without warning, it would surface in the most unexpected places with such intensity. I was once again caught between sorrow and distress.

Tragically, new memories started to surface, ones I had long buried like memories from my high school years which dated back before I decided to choose abortion. It was senior year 4 months before graduation. My closest friend came to me during school, and her face in tears. She had just found out that she was pregnant. She said that it was the first time that she ever had sex and was stunned that this happened. She was panic- stricken and frightened. My friend told me that she was afraid that her father would kill her if he found out.

At that time, abortion was illegal. Trying to be what I thought was a good friend; I told her that I knew a guy who arranged a back street abortion for his girlfriend. She asked if I could speak with him and find out if one could be arranged for her. I contacted him and the arrangements were quickly made. It was decided that my friend and I would stay at his apartment on the appointed afternoon, and a woman would come to perform the abortion. I remember asking my girlfriend that day if she was sure that she wanted to do this. She said that she was positive.

It was about a 20 minute ride to this guy's apartment. I could not believe that we were doing this - two Catholic high school senior girls spending our Saturday afternoon this way. We drove up the driveway to his building. He was standing there waiting for us. Shortly after, the woman to perform the abortion arrived. When we were introduced, she asked, "How far into the pregnancy are you?" My girlfriend told her that she was in the first trimester. The woman explained the procedure and then told her the cost. She wanted payment up front. While my girlfriend was paying her in cash, the guy walked out of his apartment. I stayed behind to be a support to my girlfriend during the procedure.

I will not go into all the gruesome details of what happened next, but I will say it was traumatic for my girlfriend and me. It affected not only our lives in ways we could never imagine, but also it damaged our long standing friendship. I withdrew from her in spite of her attempts to try to maintain our previous closeness. She felt grateful to me for helping her. I on the other hand felt ashamed of my participation in her abortion and the horror of what happened that day. I could not reconcile it. Through my partaking in her abortion, I had opened the door to evil and then began to drift into the beginning of a self destructive life course.

It was interesting to me how deeply I was able to bury and repress for

27 years something as harrowing as my friend's abortion. It was not until after I recalled this memory that I made the association of this event with the distinct decline of my moral values. Here is where I recognized for the first time the far reaching tentacles of the sin of abortion. Any association with it had poisoned my life and sent me into a downward spiral.

After recalling this, I went to confession as soon as possible to repent of my involvement in my friend's abortion. I could not wait to get rid of the guilt. My relief was short lived, and the months ahead were filled with many dark days for me. I continued to call out to Our Lady for her aid; I needed her desperately to help me bear all this sorrow. It was as though a floodgate that had held back painful memories had been opened from the moment that I saw Jesus holding my children in his arms. I knew that she was with me but could not understand why there was no relief for me from these past sins. In spite of my feelings of discouragement, I remained faithful in talking with her. I asked Our Lady to lead me out of what seemed to be an endless sorrow.

I know Our Lord in his vast mercy never reveals more truth than I can bear. I believe that it was through the intercession of Our Lady that he provided a road for me to follow which would lead me to him. He knew that I was searching for the path to experience some minimal relief from this now constant aching in my heart.

Fortunately for me, I was scheduled to attend an upcoming home school mothers' weekend retreat. The priest, Father Pedro, who would be directing the retreat, was someone I met several times before at other home school functions. I looked forward to this weekend away as possible place of solace. On my drive to the retreat, I was alone and prayed once again to Our Lady for her help to see and understand what the Lord wanted me to know.

When I entered the retreat house, I felt uncomfortable as soon as I saw Father Pedro. There was something about his presence that intimidated me. He was not responsible for these feelings through his behavior; rather, it was my own awareness of my sinfulness that made me feel self conscious. This was because I had recalled yet another memory of when abortion touched my life that I had not confessed. This memory was a situation that occurred when a close male relative came to me with his pregnant girlfriend. They wanted to abort their baby and had no money for the procedure. He asked if I could help them. I can still see his girlfriend's petrified face - her eyes pleading with me to find another way. I made the arrangements for them and paid for the abortion. We never spoke about it again even until now.

During the weekend retreat, there was an opportunity for the sacrament of reconciliation. I became terrified to go to the sacrament because of my shame over helping my close relative have an abortion. I was growing weary of sporadically confessing all these sins of abortion. Dreadfully, I entered the room for confession. There sat two oversized comfortable chairs in a dimly lit room. Although the room looked warm and inviting, my body trembled and terror filled me. I said to Father Pedro, "I am so afraid." He asked, "Why, you know me?" My fear came from my shame over my participation once again in abortion. Speaking with him face to face was extremely difficult. I had to trust Our Lady and asked for her help to reveal this to Father. I began to confess my sins in an unsteady voice, and then he absolved me. When I got up to leave and walked to the door, I stopped and turned to him. In a casual manner, I said, "Oh, I almost forgot. I did help a close male relative and his girlfriend have an abortion. I arranged it and gave them the money." Father responded in a serious tone, "Come and sit down. I need to absolve you again and give you a new penance." As I sat back down he absolved me and told me that for my penance, I was to donate the amount of money that it cost for the abortion to a Pro-Life organization. I felt embarrassed and ashamed as I quickly left the room.

Later on that evening as I lay in bed, thoughts about the penance of which I was given kept bothering me. I felt mortified having to reveal to my husband that I helped this male relative and his girlfriend get an abortion and that I paid for it. To ask my husband to pay several hundred dollars for a sin that I committed long before I met him was not right. I knew that he would be willing to do anything for me but this was something that I could not bring myself to ask him. Now, I had to do something which I had never done before - to ask a priest to change my penance.

The next morning was the last day of the retreat. I was nervous about approaching Father Pedro. I asked him if we could speak privately. We went into a quiet room and I explained my dilemma to him. Father eased my concern by changing my penance to volunteering time at a ministry in my church for an amount of time equal to the money spent on the abortion. I felt relieved and thought how hard can that be?

After the retreat, I was anxious to do the penance Father Pedro gave me as soon as possible. I immediately began to research the ministries at my church. I had to find something manageable for me, since I was a home school mom and found the responsibilities of this so demanding. There was a ministry in my parish called The Respect Life Ministry. The meetings were held only once a month, on a Friday evening. This was perfect, as my home school week ended on Friday. One of the long time members of the Respect Life committee was a woman in my parish who I had known for years. I approached her about wanting to join this committee. I did not reveal to her that this was my penance; I just expressed a desire to work in the Respect Life ministry. She told me that she did not think that they were accepting any new committee members at this time. My heart sank since I thought this was the best solution for my penance. Seeing my disappointment, she offered to ask the president of the committee if he would allow another member. Shortly after our conversation, she phoned me and said that she spoke with the president. She told me that he had agreed to let me join the committee. I felt relieved as I wanted to get this penance over with. My involvement would be short-lived because I merely wanted to volunteer to "pay back" for my offense. I had no real commitment to this ministry or what it represented.

The first meeting came quickly. Committee members gathered excitedly to discuss the night's agenda. The committee's president reintroduced the new retreat that would be held at our parish in a month. This retreat was designed for women who had experienced abortion. The Respect Life committee was asked to be responsible for all the cooking and serving of food for the retreatants during the weekend. The president then delegated all the tasks. The woman who I knew on the committee was asked to be in charge of the Sunday meal. I was not asked to do anything as this project had already been in progress before I joined the committee. My tension eased when I knew my involvement for this event would not be required.

Several weeks had passed, and my life seemed to be gaining some normalcy when one Friday, I received a phone call from the woman who I knew on the Respect Life committee. She asked me if I could help in the kitchen this Sunday, the last day of the post abortive retreat. I really wanted to say no, but I knew that I could not. I dreaded going to this place where these women were gathered to deal with their abortions. Helping

15

this cause at a distance was fine but direct involvement would be too close for comfort.

The next two days, I felt consumed by tension, irritability, and stress. When Sunday arrived, I pushed myself to get dressed while thinking of a hundred excuses that I could use to cancel. If this were not a penance I would have found a way out of it. Knowing this was a penance and wanting to complete it, I forced myself to go. Fearfully, I drove to the retreat house that morning.

I was welcomed with hugs and warm greetings from the team members. Anxiety was filling every part of my body as I thought, "What if they knew I am post abortive. They must never find out. I can keep this secret." Although I had just arrived, I was steadily watching the hands of the kitchen clock to reach the time I was scheduled to leave. I thought, "I deserve this penance, and it should be painful." I hoped that no one could read my thoughts through my expressions. My fear of being found out now matched my anxiety. I spoke little and kept myself busy with setting the table, preparing food, and cleaning dishes. There was a constant hum of conversation among the team. They kept commenting on what a privilege it was to serve these post-abortive women.

The dining room was adjacent to the kitchen, separated only by a swinging white door. The kitchen team was told not to enter the dining room while the retreatants were present. We could hear the women gathering to sit for breakfast. Squeals of delight over the bountiful meal rewarded the kitchen team who promptly hid out of sight. The murmur of conversation and clicking utensils came through the kitchen door. Shortly after, the retreat director came into the kitchen and invited the entire kitchen team to come out to the dining room. I followed the team, lingering in the back with my head hung low. All the retreatants began to sing a loud cheer for the kitchen team. When I looked up and saw the faces of these mourning women, shame covered me. Feeling embarrassed and humiliated, I thought, "I am on the wrong side of this room. It is I who should be sitting with these post-abortive women."

My once hum drum simple life had now unraveled into this complex existence. In addition to my shame and sorrow, I was now starting to experience the feeling of constant terror. There was no rational reason for this terror. I lived in a safe area and had a loving protective husband.

Nevertheless, I was terrified to be alone - always feeling frightened that something awful was going to happen to me. I was starting to have horrific visual experiences of demons following me. Fear had now become my constant companion. I thought, "How do I begin to sort out what is happening within me? Fear and shame are constantly in my thoughts!" I felt as though my life was falling apart, and I had no clue how to pull it back together. Clinging to the Blessed Mother, I would beg her to help me as I prayed the rosary. I was walking blindly in faith with her to find that peace I desperately needed.

I decided to make an appointment with Father Pedro, the priest from my home school mother's retreat, to see if he could help me. When we met, I did not initially mention anything to him about my abortions. Instead, I began our conversation with the most pressing issue for me, which was this constant feeling of terror I was experiencing. At the time, I had no awareness that many of these emotions of shame, regret, and now terror were the result of post trauma from my abortions and all these memories that had recently surfaced. I told Father Pedro that this terror was paralyzing, and I could not escape it. Then, I told him what was intensifying it were these visual experiences that I was having throughout the day. "Father, I see the faces of what I would imagine demons to look like. I feel terrified Father, what is happening to me?" I was scared and confused and felt as though I was losing my mind. I did not even get to the part of all the regret and shame which I felt over my sins of abortion when Father Pedro immediately got up and started to sprinkle the room and me with Holy Water. Then he said, "You have unrepented sin. You need to make a general confession." I asked him, "What is that?" He told me to review my life. He said, "Try to recall all the sins you committed as far back as you can remember, spending a week to examine your conscience, and then come back and I will hear your confession." Immediately, I thought, "A week, doesn't he realize that is an eternity for me in this emotional state?" His action was immediate, and he did not seem to want to continue our conversation. He wanted me to prepare well for a general confession before we proceeded further.

I left that appointment dismayed feeling rejected, confused, and alone. It was humiliating and difficult for me to reveal to him that I was having these horrible visual experiences. I felt like a really bad and evil person, especially when he got up and began shaking holy water all around. I'm certain that I probably alarmed him with my description of seeing demons.

His immediate response of grabbing holy water made me lose trust in him because I felt he was more frightened than I was. In hindsight, I think that I would have done the same thing if someone said to me that they were having demonic visions. Nevertheless, I didn't feel safe with him anymore and knew that I would not go back to see Father Pedro. I cried for a week, feeling so lost and consumed by my emotions.

Father Pedro did follow up with me and called me in a week to see if I was okay. My phone conversation with him made it seem that everything was okay even though it was not. I could not let myself open up to him in any way - I felt too vulnerable and could not allow myself to trust him with my emotions. However, I did take his advice about a general confession seriously and I spent more than one week thinking about my past sins. I made a list and carried it in my wallet. For two weeks, I walked around quite dysfunctional in great emotional pain. I felt like I was caught in a maze of confusion and fear. Continually, I beseeched Our Lady to intercede for me and to lead me to where I needed to go. It was as though God was allowing me to be held still in this emotional pain to help prepare me to be disposed to the graces that would come through my future spiritual director.

"Who can I possibly trust with these private thoughts I dare not say aloud?" I asked her. I needed help and did not know who to turn to. In a desperate attempt for relief from this constant emotional pain, I felt prompted to make an appointment with the newly assigned priest to my parish, Father Josiah. I had seen him just a few times, and he appeared to be a gentle and holy man. I knew that it was imperative to speak with a priest. I could no longer bear this alone.

As I hesitantly entered the room, Father Josiah greeted me with such warmth. Our meeting began by telling him of my experience with the priest, Father Pedro, from my retreat. I shared what I revealed about the demonic visions and how Father Pedro sprinkled the room with Holy Water and me as well. "You have unrepented sin," he said, "You need to thoroughly examine your conscience and make a general confession." I also told Father Josiah about the penance given to me by Father Pedro to volunteer time in ministry service equal to the amount of money spent on the abortion. Then, I described the one day that I volunteered at the post abortive retreat on the kitchen team and how I felt. I said, "I know that I am a sensitive person, and I'm sure that I'm taking this all too personally, yet I can't stop crying, and I still feel devastated after my meeting with Father Pedro." My sadness came pouring out, and the tears steadily steamed down my face as I spoke. Father Josiah sat there for a moment, and then he began to speak softly. "I apologize for that priest on your retreat and any priest that may have hurt you. That penance given to you of ministry service should have had limits put on it and not been left up to you to decide what would be a sufficient amount of time to volunteer your service. Do you think that service on the kitchen team that day fulfilled you penance?" "No", I said. Father Josiah replied "Sometimes, another can take on one's penance," and then he asked if he could take my penance by contributing the money spent on the abortion on my behalf. I was stunned by his generosity. "No, Father, this is something that I need to do." It was obvious that Father Josiah was concerned about how far I would take this.

This idea about making a general confession was pressing on me. I asked Father Josiah if I already confessed all the sins I can remember why would I need to do it again. Weren't these sins already forgiven? He assured me that they were forgiven and explained that sometimes sorrow for past sins becomes greater as time goes on, and one may feel a need to readdress these sins. I am a scrupulous person and wanted to readdress my sins. I knew that my sorrow had deepened since I had originally confessed many of these sins. Needing to be freed from all these debilitating emotions, I had great hope that this general confession would give me the graces for this to be accomplished. I asked Father if he would hear my general confession. He agreed and told me to examine my conscience. He left the room for awhile to allow me private time.

When Father returned, I felt so frightened and ashamed after looking at the long list I had compiled of all the sins during my life that I could remember. Father Josiah said, "Are you ready?" as he pulled his chair up. My voice shaking, I began recounting all my offenses. Father listened and guided me through my general confession, especially during the part when I confessed my abortions. There, he helped me to understand that I was still not viewing the truth about the gift God had given me in the children who he sent me. This happened when I made a comment after I confessed the abortions. I said, "Well, at least the fathers of my aborted babies are no longer in my life because of my abortions, and now that whole period of my life is over." After that comment, Father Josiah in a gentle manner brought me back again to the truth by saying, "The Blessed Mother was standing by you as you were lying upon that table during your abortions."

19

Immediately, I felt the shame of what I had done before my heavenly mother. I thought, "Why would he say such a riveting statement?" Then he proceeded by saying, "Teresa you are as much a mother today to those children as the day you aborted them." He was right. My heavenly mother never abandoned me under any circumstances, so why was I abandoning my aborted children. I was still thinking about my motherhood to my aborted children as a past event through the rationalizations that I wanted to hold onto. I wondered if Father Josiah realized the hope that he infused into my soul at that moment with those words. "You are still a mother today to those children." His courage as well as boldness to say this statement on the lips of love pulled me back into the truth. Within the grace of this sacrament, this priest sitting before me in the person of Christ reflected the true essence of what healing would be for me - it was to reclaim my motherhood. I immediately felt hope and thought, "I am still a mother to these children. This is incomprehensible! Could I have a second chance?" Even though I did not fully understand what that meant, I knew something extraordinary just happened through the words of Father Josiah. Then Father said those healing words, "I absolve you from all these sins and any sins you have ever committed in your life." All I could recollect was emptied out before Father Josiah and forgiven now leaving room within my soul for the real truth and abundant grace to enter. I felt free and thoroughly cleansed.

Insights I received through General Confession:

I learned that any trace or connection to this sin of abortion had to be rooted out. This sin was like a spiritual cancer. The process to do this for me was general confession with Father Josiah. By reviewing my life sins and sincerely repenting them aloud to a priest, it pulled this sin of abortion out from its root. It eliminated its long reaching tentacles which fed off of deceit that continually seized my thoughts and sense of reason.

After going through this experience, I deeply appreciated Father Pedro's wisdom in suggesting that I make a general confession. How could he have possibly known that I needed to recount those sins again to remove their power of guilt from me? His words, "You have unrepented sin," were true. I marvel over the fact that he recognized the signs, and I believe that it was the grace of his vocation which gave him this insight. He was right - I needed to bring back past offenses, some of which I had not confessed and others which I confessed poorly in the past. I am grateful to Father Pedro for pointing me in this direction.

I now have a great love and appreciation for the sacrament of reconciliation and its healing power to overcome the effects of sin. After my general confession, not only did my thoughts and feelings move from despair to great hope, but I also never again experienced those demonic visions. The humiliation and brokenness which I felt opened the way for grace to fill me.

Lastly, Father Josiah in the person of Christ through the grace of his vocation helped me to deeply desire becoming as much a mother today to my children as the day I aborted them. This sacramental experience was pivotal in my healing. Through grace, I was no longer focusing on regret and shame but looking toward my future with hope of reclaiming my motherhood. This seed of hope would grow into a relationship with my aborted children that I never imagined possible.

FOLLOWING THE SHEPHERD

" They caught me, sorrow and distress. I called on the Lord's name. O Lord my God, deliver me!"
Psalm 116

This fourth transition to healing was immediate. Having received sacramental and sanctifying graces through a general confession, I was opened and disposed to follow the voice of the shepherd even though this would mean going through the dark valley of death. I had confidence and trust in Father Josiah because he was a priest. He was in Persona Christi and his concern reflected this divine love.

The events on the road of following the shepherd:

After my general confession that Sunday evening, Father Josiah asked, "Can you stay awhile longer?" I felt confused as I just finished confession and thought this is finally over. Even though almost an hour and a half of conversation had already passed, I could see the genuine concern on his face to speak more. Unbeknown to me, Father was a trained Project Rachel counselor. Project Rachel, as you know, is a Catholic ministry that provides one-on-one post-abortive counseling and reconciliation to individuals who are suffering from the traumatic effects of abortion. He recognized the need for me to go through the necessary healing process. Father Josiah began to explain Project Rachel, and it would take several sessions to go through it. There were different stages of healing: the first of which we had just done through sacrament of reconciliation. Now, he wanted to move quickly to the second step.

His words whirled in an incoherent fog. I thought to myself, "Why can't I just leave now and see if my life would resume normalcy? How many more steps did I need to go through? Wasn't this enough?" I was emotionally exhausted.

Father Josiah was so gentle and loving as he spoke to me about the necessity to stay longer. He thought that it would be wise for me to move to the next stage now because I just finished confession. Father Josiah knew that left on my own; there would be a risk that I would not fully embrace my motherhood to my aborted children and my dignity in Christ. I was still too fragile. I felt trust with Father, so I consented to stay awhile longer that Sunday night. Little did I know that this would be my first step in faith on the road to meeting my aborted children.

Father explained that the next step was for me to tell him about my life story - any significant events that I could remember, especially about the abortions. I clearly recall how nausea welled up in me as memories raced through my head. My throat tightened as my heart sped. I looked at him with fear, but his eyes were filled with gentleness and love. Amazingly, I felt safe with him and began to walk through the past 45 years of my life. My life had been difficult and filled with many traumatic experiences, and I wept in bitter sorrow as I spoke, experiencing again all the pain as I visited each old memory.

When I finished my story, Father's face was full of compassion, and his eyes filled with tears. I had never shared all these details of my past with anyone but my husband and that was done over time - not in one conversation. I felt raw and exposed. Father knew that I had emptied myself out before him, and he reassured me that all I had confided in him would be kept private. He forewarned me that I would be feeling vulnerable for a while and encouraged me to stop at our church's Perpetual Eucharistic Adoration Chapel on my way out. He blessed me and said, "Go spend time with Jesus".

I walked across the parking lot to the path that led to the chapel. That night was the first time that the words on the sign which hung by the door spoke deeply to my heart: "Come to me all you who are weary and find life burdensome I will refresh you." Slowly I opened the door and could see the dim flicker of the candles burning. I craved the peace that filled the room, but it was not penetrating me. I felt broken and exhausted. I kept chanting to myself, "I believe. I believe," as I thought, "I need you, Jesus, to help me through this post-abortive healing. I believe you can although I don't know how." After ten minutes, I left. I walked to my car through the brisk night air. I was grateful for the camouflage of the darkness that had fallen. Mindlessly, I drove not remembering the streets which I rode down or the turns which I made to get home. I sat in front of my house dazed and drained. I could only think of seeing my husband's face. He is my best friend, and his arms are a safe abode for me. As I opened the front door, he was anxiously waiting on the other side. I had been gone for hours, and he was concerned. I could not speak and fell into his arms in tears. Finally, I said, "There's something that we need to talk about - it's called Project Rachel."

That following morning, I reflected on my time with Father Josiah. I started to think about my life story. It was as though a fog had been lifted from my mind. The grace of reconciliation had given me a mental clarity about myself. I was now able to identify how my past actions had been influenced by this sin of abortion.

I realized that when I made the decision to help my high school friend acquire an abortion, it was that decision which primed me to become open to the idea of abortion as an option. The guilt which I had felt from helping my friend had driven me to amputate any healthy relationships in my life. I isolated myself and the shame that I felt pulled me away from the church and the sacraments that would have put me on the right path. Sin then escalated in my life by making one bad choice after another which resulted in self destructive behavior - from sexual promiscuity to drug and alcohol abuse. The roots of that sin of abortion were driven into my core. I had been tormented by the consequences of this sin like no other that I had committed. Although I felt relieved to have such a heighten awareness, I was not prepared for the level of dysfunction that would soon follow.

I was now conscious of the necessity of post-abortive healing. It was becoming clear to me through the unpredictability of my emotional and psychological state. I was anxious to meet with Father Josiah for our second Project Rachel counseling session about a week later. So much had unraveled in a week for me emotionally. I discussed my concern about the level of dysfunction which I was starting to experience in my daily routine with Father Josiah. Being a home school mother meant I had to be able to parent as well as educate my children. My regular schedule of school lesson planning, teaching, and carrying out household tasks had now become too difficult to manage. The enormity of the sadness about my abortions and not knowing my aborted children was robbing me of my ability to concentrate. My aborted children were now in the forefront of my mind. Although my despair had vanished, it was now replaced with this inexplicable longing for my aborted babies. I wanted to be their mother, I needed to have that second chance of still being their mother today as the day I aborted them.

I asked Father Josiah if it was possible for me to attend a post-abortive weekend retreat. I expressed my desire for a faster more concentrated healing process. I foolishly thought that this healing could be accomplished in a weekend, not understanding that a wound of this nature would take time - God's time.

Father was open to the idea and told me there was a post-abortive retreat coming up in six months at another parish in a neighboring state. I thought, "A six month wait, I can't be in this emotional state for six months!" I asked him if there would be any other retreats held sooner. He said that there would be one held in our parish in several weeks. Seeing the relief on my face, Father became concerned about my obvious interest in this retreat and that it would be in our parish. He said that he did not recommend attending this type of retreat in my home parish. Father told me that there would be too many emotional risks involved for me.

Deep within, I knew Father was right about the risks, yet my frantic desire for peace and normalcy consumed me. I knew that if I decided to attend this particular retreat, I would need to take into account my family's feelings along with my own. We had been visibly active in our church community for eight years. I did not want to cause pain or embarrassment for my family. In addition to this, many parishioners whom my family knew would be involved with running this retreat, making true anonymity impossible. The risk for breech of confidentiality would be greater in this situation. I told Father that I would consider his concern, but I wanted to pray about this option. Father encouraged me in my choice to pray about it.

I did pray daily about attending this retreat in my parish. My desire to get out of this emotional discomfort overrode everything. What was attractive to me was that the retreat offered a window of time without distractions for me to grieve the loss of my children openly. I had just begun to build a trusting relationship with Father Josiah and felt the presence of Jesus' love through him. I was torn between following Father and my pressing need for immediate emotional relief. I sacrificed the security of his involvement and his fatherly guidance, and I decided to attend the retreat.

Insights that I learned through following the shepherd:

I did receive heightened self awareness about my openness to sin through the different choices I made. Telling all the painful details of my life aloud brought them outside of me. That allowed me to view them and took much of the power of helplessness away from me. When sharing a story of shame with all the details, it opens the darkness of a soul to another. This is sacred ground and requires a reverence on the part of the listener. Intuitively, I understood when I sat before a priest that all I shared would be held within a scared confidentiality. There would be no judgment, nor would I be treated any differently whenever we would see one another. It would be the same as when I confess my sins while participating in reconciliation. The charism of the priesthood would provide that security. A priest would never allude to my sins in any form outside of confession nor spiritual counseling. There is no substitute for a priest.

Unfortunately, although many are well intentioned, they do not have the grace a priest has to protect the dignity of a soul. There is a risk that the bond of confidentiality and non-judgment, although promised, could not be possible in the retreat setting. I strayed from the voice of the shepherd, Father Josiah, who tried to warn me. Nevertheless, God would use even those unfortunate circumstances for his glory.

Lastly, I also experienced a deep understanding of the story in Matthew 18 where Jesus speaks about the lost sheep. The man left his 99 other sheep to find the one who strayed. Father Josiah's generosity of time and concern for me made me feel as though he was claiming me as his own spiritual child whom he was leading to a place of safety. Even though I went against his advice, he still decided to remain involved. I felt like the lost sheep that the shepherd left the other 99 behind to find. Through his constant reassurance, I was able to receive the spiritual favors and consolations that God wished to grant as a way to build a relationship with my children. Father's decision to stay involved with my healing process was critical for me.

THE IMPORTANCE OF A NAME

"In waiting and in calm you shall be saved in quiet and in trust your strength lies"

Isaiah 30

The fifth phase was discovering the significance of a name. I knew names were important to God through the beautiful scripture stories, which I have read. Names held identity and information about the person. An example is in the scripture story when the angel Gabriel greeted Mary and called her "Hail full of grace" instead of Mary. This was her identity and how she was viewed by God. When Jesus changed Simon's name to Peter this was his identity as seen by Jesus. Peter was the rock of the church, the first pope. When God changed Abram's name to Abraham, he saw him as the father of nations. However, the meaning of names for God didn't really impact me until it touched my own life. Here in my fifth stage of healing, I experience for the first time my dignity as a mother to my aborted children through their names.

The events that led up to discovering the importance of names:

I registered for the post-abortive retreat and was sent a letter of things to expect on the weekend. One of the things recommended was to be prepared to name my aborted children. It was important to me to select meaningful names for my children, but not knowing their sex made this difficult. I was frustrated by the fact that I had not paid closer attention to their genders when I had that visual prayer experience of seeing Jesus holding them in his arms at the gate. My constant worry about what to name them was weighing me down. I had less than two and a half weeks to decide.

My husband, seeing my anxiety, advised me to go to our Perpetual Adoration chapel to seek my answers there. I committed to go before Our

Eucharistic Lord every day until the retreat arrived. I beseeched the Blessed Mother for her help. Each day, I would pray my rosary before the Blessed Sacrament, feeling confident that I would receive what I needed. However, after a week, I became concerned as their names still remained unknown to me. I was determined to be faithful to my commitment and continued to pray with hope.

Then one day on my way into the chapel, I saw on a table in the hallway a pamphlet. It was a 9 day novena to St. Therese. I was familiar with her, and that she was known for her "little way". I had heard that when she intercedes on behalf of a person, if God grants the intention prayed for, St. Therese will send roses on the ninth day of the novena. I really did not pray to the saints. Occasionally, I would pray to Saint Anthony to help me find things. Aside from that, my prayers were directed to Jesus and Mary. Yet, at this moment, I felt compelled to pick up the pamphlet. I thought, "Why not? I can use all the help I can get. It can't hurt," so I grabbed the pamphlet and decided to pray the 9 day novena for St. Therese's help. I asked her to intercede on my behalf for the names of my children.

The night before the retreat arrived, while I was packing my clothes for the weekend, I reflected on the past week. I started to feel resentful because I still had not yet received the names for my children. Even though there were still a couple of days left until I completed the novena, my confidence in St. Therese had begun to waver. How could I attend this retreat and not be able to name my children? Frustrated and angry, I tried to re-direct my thoughts to whatever possibilities would lie ahead at the retreat.

The Friday night and Saturday afternoon of the retreat had allowed me the space which I hoped to grieve the loss of my children. I had just ended my novena to Saint Therese that Saturday morning and felt disappointed that I still had no names to give my children. I tried to resist this distraction of feeling let down by her.

On that Saturday evening of the retreat after dinner, all the retreatants were asked to gather in the upper room. As I opened the door, I was struck by the beauty of the room. It was bathed in candlelight. A large coffee table covered with rose petals sat in the center of the room. Nestled among the petals were several rows of unlit candles. Immediately, my heart started to race as I hoped those rose petals were a sign that my novena to Saint

Therese was answered.

It was unannounced beforehand that this was the appointed time in the retreat that we would be asked to participate in a ritual of naming our children. We were instructed to get up one at a time, walk to the coffee table in the center of the room, and light a candle while saying aloud our child's name. The facilitator added that we were also to name any children lost through miscarriage. I immediately became alarmed by this as I thought about the pregnancy which occurred between my two abortions. It was an ectopic pregnancy in which my child died. I thought, "Oh no, I'm struggling with names for my two aborted children, and now it is necessary for me to decide another name for my baby lost in the ectopic pregnancy!" Shaken by the need to choose another child's name, I quickly prayed again to St. Therese and Our Lady for help. I nervously watched as the women stood up one at a time to light the candles and name their children. I sat in secret hope of knowing what to name mine. Time seemed to move so quickly as I watched the majority of women name their children. I had to make a decision, there was no time left, and it was my turn. Even though we were all told right before the ceremony that we could wait until after the retreat to decide upon names, I did not want to be the only mother leaving the retreat with nameless children. I felt too ashamed to do that.

I disappointedly stood up and resigned myself to select any names for them. Walking with my head down, I dejectedly reached for the long, thin, wooden stick to light the first candle. At the moment when the flame ignited the stick, I heard a name whispered in my mind, Michelle Marie. I lovingly said her name as I lit the candle. My hand began to tremble as I went to light the second candle because again, I heard a name whispered Ezekiel James. Tears of gratitude made it difficult for me to light the third candle when I heard yet another name whispered, Daniel John. I was astounded that my prayer had actually been answered and slowly sat in my chair. The priest sitting next to me asked, "What made you choose the name Ezekiel?" "I didn't", I said. He looked confused. I explained to the priest about my novena to St. Therese. I told him that I did not even know how to spell Ezekiel. The priest smiled and spelled my son's name for me. I leaned back proudly and thought, "I have daughter and two sons." Filled with awe, I thanked Saint Therese, Our Lady, and Our Lord for introducing me to my children.

In describing to you now the conditions prior to the abortions of my children, it will provide for you an appreciation of the meaning of their names, their identities, as well as mine in the eyes of an all merciful God. Through this information, I think you will get a glimpse of why their given names held such significance.

My first child, Michelle Marie:

When I was 18 years old, I had left home. I had a very tumultuous relationship with my parents. I did not feel any confidence or trust in them. I felt repeatedly betrayed by the way that they chose to handle certain conflicts which we had at home. After I graduated high school, I decided to move out, and a male friend that I knew offered to let me stay with him, as I could not yet support myself. It did not take long before I became pregnant by him. Upon hearing the news that I was pregnant, he made it clear that he did not want the child.

I wanted my baby, so I decided to approach my Mother for help, in spite of our estrangement from one another. When I told her that I was pregnant, she looked at me with great disappointment and disgust. She said, "You have to have an abortion!" Being raised Catholic; I thought that she would help me because an abortion was out of the question for our religion. I knew that she would be upset with me, but I never expected that she would want me to abort my baby. Her response devastated me. I immediately left the house and knew I was on my own.

I did not hear from my Mom again regarding this matter. I was unaware of the fact at the time that my Mother never told my Dad that I was pregnant. When I did not hear from my Father as well during that time, I realized how truly alone I was in assuming this responsibility. Hoping to discover a way to keep my child, I waited a couple of months trying to find a solution. However, I knew I was not able to support myself financially nor could I return home or depend on the baby's father. I felt terrified and thought that I had no choice but to abort my child.

Abortion had just become legal in New York. I reluctantly decided to go to the Manhattan clinic and abort my daughter Michelle Marie. This action on my part crushed any sense of esteem that I had. I felt distraught by my choice. I despised myself for being such a coward who would kill her own child.

My first child's name is Michelle Marie which means (Michelle) one who is like God (Marie) Sympathetic. When I learned the meaning of my daughter's name, I thought about how much God loves me to give me that name for her. It was as though God was saying to me, "Teresa, I am God, your father, who is sympathetic to you, my child." It reassured me that God knew my heart, and I had reluctantly aborted my daughter. He saw that I felt lost and alone. He knew the sorrow that I felt over the decision to abort her. Even though I committed this serious sin, his sympathy for me, my situation, and my wrong choice was present. I then thought about my daughter, Michelle Marie. She must be like God in this way, compassionate and sympathetic, or why else would he give her that name? I believe Michelle Marie is tender hearted and has great love for me like God, her Father.

My second child, Ezekiel James:

I became pregnant for the second time when I was 21 years old with my son. It had been four years since I had aborted his sister, Michelle Marie. After aborting my daughter, I quickly spun into a self-destructive pattern. I moved from one abusive relationship to another. Sexual promiscuity, drugs, and alcohol became my standard mode of operation for years. I had been living a life which totally rejected God. My world was consumed with darkness, and I lived in grave sin. My soul was in jeopardy as I had continued to break every commandment. Everyday, I had spiraled further down into self-hate and frequently entertained thoughts of suicide. My desire to die almost became a reality.

One late Saturday morning, I began to experience this unbearable physical pain in my abdominal area. It was so severe that I decided to call my older sister who lived nearby for help. She took me to the emergency room, and the doctor sent me home with the diagnosis of a stomach virus. As the day went on, the pain continued to escalate. My sister stayed at my bedside and by evening, I was going into shock. This time, when she brought me back to the emergency room, the shifts had changed, and another doctor was on duty. After examining me, the doctor admitted me for emergency surgery. He said, "Honey, I do not know what is wrong, but I have to open you up now to find out."

My sister had called my parents and notified them of the seriousness of my condition. They arrived as I was being wheeled toward the operating room. My mother had seen a priest in the hallway and asked him to come with her to see me. The priest walked up to the gurney, and he began praying over me. I thought that he was giving me last rites, so I started screaming, "Get him away from me." I was scared because I sensed that I was dying. Now that I was faced with what seemed to be death, I realized that I really did not want to die after all. But because of that priest's presence at that moment, I was reminded about God, someone who I never talked to or thought about. Upon the idea of God entering my mind through the persona of that priest, I began to pray. I cried out from the depths of my heart as I entered the operating room, "God if you let me live, I promise I will do whatever I can to find you."

The doctor told me after the surgery that I had barely escaped death. My fallopian tube had ruptured and I was hemorrhaging internally. In spite of my regular use of a diaphragm for contraception, I had become pregnant for the second time. This pregnancy was an ectopic pregnancy. The doctor explained that he had to remove my fallopian tube and a quarter of my uterus. He said that I had less than 20 percent chance of becoming pregnant, and if I did, it would be a high risk pregnancy. I found out later that a serious infection, which resulted immediately after my first abortion caused this severe damage to my fallopian tube. The scarring of my tube prevented the embryo from reaching the uterus, so it was forced to grow inside my fallopian tube. This fatal situation caused the death of my son, Ezekiel James. God in his mercy spared me and allowed me to survive. My life was given to me for a second chance.

After my recuperation, I tried to search for God as I had promised him. All my efforts were unsuccessful as I still felt very disconnected from God. My mother made some attempts to encourage me by suggesting several times that I attend a Catholic retreat called Cursillo which was being held in our area. I reluctantly took her advice and went to the retreat. While I was there, it was wonderful. Seeds of faith were planted.

My second child's name Ezekiel James means (Ezekiel) God is strong (James) he who supplants, uproot in order to replace with something else. The trauma of this near death experience opened my mind and heart to seek God. Through that search for him my life of immorality and serious sin was uprooted and replaced with a desire for God. My life would never be the same. Instead of a running away from God, I would feel unrest without him, a longing to know him. God in his might and mercy saved me, and he did it through the life given up for me, my son, Ezekiel James. I believe that this was as the scripture says, "No one has greater love than this, to lay down one's life for one's friends" (John 15:13). I am assured of my son's love for me and the price of that love.

My third child, Daniel John:

My third pregnancy occurred when I was 24 years old. I had been trying to live a Christian life. Although I had not returned to the sacramental life of the Catholic Church I was involved with an Evangelical Church that I attended several times a week. There, I received some nourishment from a weekly bible study. In spite of my efforts, I still felt tempted by my old lifestyle of immorality and found it hard to resist my previous boyfriend of the past four years who continued to pursue me. I did not have the spiritual strength to stay away from that relationship knowing it went against the teaching of Jesus. Eventually, it became too hard to love God and reject this man who I thought loved me. I wanted the satisfaction of that human relationship instead. I decided to push God far into the background and live with my boyfriend.

It seemed to have paid off because he proposed to me, and we planned to marry. He was my world, and all my self-worth was from this relationship with him. When I found out that I was pregnant, we were both excited about having a child. After three months into the pregnancy, my fiancé changed his mind about wanting our baby and left me. He would not return unless I aborted our child. I was devastated. I knew that I could not support my child alone. Once again, I approached family who I trusted and found no support from them. Afraid to face this responsibility alone and even more frightened to lose the relationship with my fiancé; I decided to do the very thing that I never thought I would ever consider again - abort my baby.

This time, it would be more complicated as I was in my second trimester, and I had a partial uterus. My son would need to be surgically removed. While waiting for my turn to go into the surgery room, I was writing a letter to my child, asking forgiveness for my cowardice. I was disgusted with myself over my lack of courage as I went ahead with my choice and aborted my son. Deep within, I knew God loved me and felt ashamed of how I was betraying him, yet I had no inner strength to change my decision.

My third child's name is Daniel John. It means (Daniel) God is my judge (John) God is gracious. You can imagine the joy and relief which I felt when I learned the meaning of my son's name. God knew all I was dealing with in my heart at the moment of Daniel John's death. God knew that I felt tormented for years after that abortion over my betrayal of his fatherly love by aborting this child which he had given me. God reminded me in my son's name that he is gracious and rich in mercy. He knew how sorry I was for this horrific act. God knew how guilty I felt about starting in relationship with him and then not having the courage or strength to resist the sins before me. In Daniel John's name, I was reassured that God alone is my judge; He alone knows the human heart and heard all that I could not verbalize.

Insights I learned through the importance of a name:

I realize now as I look back at that time of my life the importance of the sacraments, especially reconciliation. During the time of my abortions, I still had not come back to the Catholic Church. There was no sacramental presence in my life. No sanctifying grace to strengthen me to make the right choices. I needed that which only the Catholic Church can give through the priest in the person of Christ. Yes, I had encountered Christ and his love, through the word, scripture studies, and the witness of others in this Evangelical Church, yet I became like the seed that fell among thorns, and the thorns grew up and choked it (Matthew 13).

I also recognized that it was only through the graces given to me by Our Lord and Our Lady that I was able to wait for the names of my children. Also, for the first time, I understood the powerful help that can come through the intercession of saints. Since this event, I have on different occasions asked a saint to walk with me through certain difficulties in my life. I now view saints as my faithful friends. This attitude has deepened my dependence upon God and my understanding that I can do nothing without grace.

Through waiting for the names of my children, I learned how important names are to God. How very much he says in a name about that person's identity. Their names not only revealed something about their character but also seemed to be a response from God of how he viewed me after the abortions and ectopic pregnancy. This was a very important part of my healing to realize that God loved me so much that he would give me the names of my children. I felt so special to God, precious in his eyes. At the same time my heart was filling with maternal pride over my sons and daughter. It felt like a rebirthing of my children. This was a moment of grace through which I was regaining my dignity as their mother - something that I hoped would happen but could not imagine how it would occur.

It was this very act of faith through the graces I received of praying and waiting for their names that was the initial stage of forming the bond between me and my aborted children. Receiving their names increased my sense of dignity as their mother as well as a daughter of God. It would impart upon me an inner strength that would become a bulwark to the constant guilt and shame that I had previously felt about my decisions to abort.

THE POWER OF THE EUCHARIST

"No one can receive anything except what has been given from heaven"

John 3

The sixth stage of healing occurred through experiencing the power of the Eucharist. How often I took Our Eucharistic Lord's presence for granted. Holy Communion became all too familiar to me. I understood the experience of consolation before Our Eucharistic Lord but not of his power. I would discover that by staying in his presence and remaining in him would be the remedy for my healing. No human ways or carefully thought out methods for post-abortive healing could restore me. It would only be the majestic presence of Our Eucharistic Lord.

The events that led to understanding the power of the Eucharist:

It was bittersweet for me to receive the names of my children. I was happy to know that I had two boys and a girl. I felt humbled that God answered my request to know what to name them, yet I felt great sorrow about never having time with my children or knowing who they were. That sadness was creeping in to overshadow my joy.

I had the opportunity to go to reconciliation that Saturday evening of the retreat after I received their names during the ritual. I felt guilty for having any sadness after the beautiful consolation which God had just given me by revealing their names. I told Father Bernard in confession that I had already confessed aborting my children, but my regret has now turned into this deep longing to be with them and to experience them even though I knew that this was impossible. I cried as I told him about this desire I felt for a relationship with my three children. Father Bernard in an effort to console me said, "Remember every time you are in the presence of Jesus, they are there too." His words comforted me, and I left confession that night feeling some reassurance and hope.

Later that Saturday evening, a sign up sheet was posted for time slots to be alone with Our Lord during Eucharistic adoration throughout the night. Only one person per hour was permitted to ensure an opportunity for private adoration. I signed up for an early morning hour eager to be alone with Our Lord. I felt so appreciative of this opportunity to be with him.

My alarm rang at 1:50 a.m. and I got up quickly to go down to the chapel for my two o'clock adoration hour. I slowly opened the heavy wooden door. The chapel was beautiful, dimly lit with only a few candles on the altar. There was just enough light to see the detailed artwork of the stained glass windows that encased the room. I felt the sacredness of this space the moment I crossed its threshold.

There on the floor right in front of the altar were three large pillows. I decided this is where I would sit. In the center of the altar there stood a beautiful monstrance. Placed about twelve inches to the left of the monstrance was a statue. It was Jesus sitting with two young boys and a girl. Jesus' arm was stretched out to the side as though He was pointing to something for the children to look at. When I saw the statue of the three children with Jesus, I immediately smiled and thought, "I have two sons and a daughter." I felt overwhelmed with gratitude to God for revealing that to me.

I began to praise Our Lord and adore him with such fervor. I thought about how much he loves me to give me the names of my children. I felt special to God, cherished by him. My heart felt as though it would burst with thanksgiving as I sat before his presence.

Then I began to stare at the statue of Jesus with the children and imagined that they were my daughter and two sons with him. I wondered what he was telling them and what he was pointing to. I noticed that here, on this altar, that statue of Jesus was pointing to the monstrance. It was as though he was saying look at the host in the monstrance. My gaze shifted back to the host. As I was looking at the Eucharist and praising him, I saw the face of a young boy appear inside the host – a face I had never seen before. I felt bewildered by what was happening while looking at the boy's face. Then, his face quickly transformed into a young girl's face - again someone I did not recognize. I felt confused and nervous, but I did not want to stop looking at the host. Then within a minute, the young girl's face transformed into another young boy's face, which again was someone that I did not recognize. Suddenly, I remembered what Father Bernard said to me just several hours earlier during confession. "Remember every time you are in the presence of Jesus, they are there too." I thought, "Could this really be happening? I know they are spiritually with Jesus, but is this possible that I can literally see them?" I could not believe my eyes and started to rub them. My heart and mind were racing with excitement. I then saw the three children together inside the host. It was a moment of tremendous grace given to me. This spiritual consolation of seeing my children continued throughout the rest of my holy hour.

During that hour, I examined their features, their smiles, and their hair. I wanted them etched into my memory forever. Interestingly, they did not appear as babies but rather as young children. This was a mystery to me. I sat there on the floor before the monstrance in awe over the fact that the Lord was allowing me this time with my children. Then I heard the door of the chapel open behind me. It was the next adorer who had signed up for her private holy hour with the Lord. With great difficulty, I slowly got up to leave the chapel. I returned to my room and laid in bed thinking about my three beautiful children and fell into a peaceful sleep.

The next morning was the closing of the retreat. There was a sharing session with feedback from all the retreatants about their weekend experience. I felt uneasy about revealing to anyone that I saw my children inside the host. I guess I did not think anyone would believe me. However, later that morning, I approached the two psychologists who were on the retreat team and decided to tell them separately what had happened to me. They were Father Bernard, who was the priest that I went to for reconciliation, and the woman, who was the retreat facilitator. I felt encouraged by their reactions as they were not surprised. The retreat facilitator told me that once during another post-abortive retreat, a woman had this same experience. The woman saw her children inside the host during her holy hour. This woman was an artist and was able to sketch the faces of her children. So evidently this type of spiritual consolation had happened for other post-abortive parents which I found reassuring.

I was anxious for the retreat to end so I could tell my husband and Father Josiah what happened during the weekend. When I returned home, I excitedly told my husband, son, and daughter that I saw the three children. I described what they looked like and told them their names. They were in awe over this spiritual consolation that I received. My husband immediately said a prayer of thanksgiving aloud as we all sat there in amazement of the power of God. It was very comforting to me that my family so readily believed me as I was still astounded that this visual experience really happened to me.

That evening I met with Father Josiah and told him everything that happened on the retreat. He was so happy for me and also easily believed all I that I shared with him. He understood the power of grace. We prayed together and thanked God for his great mercy upon me.

> *"The more God wishes to bestow on us, the more does he make us desire"*
>
> Saint John of the Cross

This reality of embracing my dignity as mother to my aborted children continued to unfold in unexpected ways. After the retreat, I felt this incredible desire to bond with my children, especially after seeing their precious faces and learning their names. My longing for them increased in spite of thoughts that I had like "Teresa, do not dare to dream about such a relationship with them! That possibility was gone forever, the moment you aborted them. You were not acting as a mother when you caused the demise of your children. You had done the most unnatural act as a mother, the most horrific - destroying their very lives. Maternal bonding had not occurred and could not, it is too late."

How could I desire more? I thought "Be satisfied that you genuinely believe God and your children forgive you. Be happy with the consolations of knowing their names and seeing their faces." That alone should have given me peace. I wanted it to; I tried hard for it to be enough, yet peace was not mine. I could not quench this growing desire to know my children. This was a mystery to me as so much had already been given me, tremendous spiritual consolations. I felt guilty for wanting more and began to think that I should have never started this healing process as I now felt worse than when I began. I felt as though something was wrong with me. This desire for bonding which I tried to resist grew in spite of the improbability of such a relationship. It was so pressing and constant that I could not stop thinking about it. Father Josiah's words in the beginning of this post-abortive journey, "You are as much a mother today to your aborted babies as the day you aborted them" kept coming back to me.

"More tortuous than all else is the human heart, beyond remedy; who can understand it?"
Jeremiah 17

Jeremiah states that only the Lord really can know the remedy. I trusted the Lord with all my heart and believed that he knew my emotional suffering over this longing I felt for a relationship with my children. I had to rely upon his grace and mercy. There was no where else to go but on my knees and pray to him and Our Lady about this. I decided to visit the perpetual Eucharistic adoration chapel at my parish everyday. Where else could I go to receive strength and understanding? So much had been stirred within my heart that I did not understand. I would go before Our Lord in the Blessed Sacrament lamenting over the loss of never knowing my aborted children. I can still hear my cry, "Please help me; help me to live with this loss of never knowing my children. Lord please take this desire away from me if it is not from you. If this desire is true and good and what God wants for me, then Our Lady, please, I beg you to help me through this. My Lord, you have given me so much; I ask one more thing, please help me to know how to handle this desire to know my children." I kept up this constant, relentless banging at the door of heaven, pleading daily with the Blessed Mother, appealing to her motherhood and saying to her, "Mother you understand a mother's heart. You know how mine is breaking. Do not abandon me - help me." This prayer opened the realm of where I unknowingly was being led by God - into relationship with my aborted children. Again grace would be provided. I was about to experience a reuniting process that began with heart wrenching sorrow and would end in unimaginable joy. Spiritual healing would close the wounds that had been opened in my heart and mind regarding my abortions. God would provide a way not only to heal these wounds but also to remove any scarring that could have remained as evidence.

What I am about to share next makes me nervous because by nature, it so personal and private. I can only tell you the truth of what happened to me; I cannot convince, nor am I trying to convince you. I just desire to do God's will and show myself fully to you, the priest, and tell you about the healing that I have received.

After the retreat during my daily visits with Our Eucharistic Lord, I went through the way of Mary. I would cling to Our Lady for her help and her intercession for me before her son. It was Lent, so I would begin my holy hour reciting the sorrowful mysteries of the rosary and meditate on Our Lady and Our Lord's suffering. I united my own emotional suffering with theirs. While praying to my great surprise, I saw my three children visibly present in the host with Jesus. I could not believe this was happening again! Why would God allow this? I remember thinking "How is this possible, Lord?" Foolishly, I thought, "This is a different chapel, a different host." As I was looking at the children inside the host, I asked the Holy Spirit and Our Lady for the grace to help me to receive this spiritual consolation openly. This was such a mystery to me. I felt excited, confused, and nervous.

Immediately after spending an hour in Eucharistic adoration at the chapel, I walked across the parking lot to the rectory. I needed to speak with my spiritual director, Father Josiah. I felt concerned about this appearance again of my children inside the host. As wonderful as it was to see my children, it was beyond anything that I imagined possible. I did try to receive this experience openly while it was happening, but I felt some level of fear. Father Josiah knew that I had seen them once during the retreat weekend. When I told Father Josiah that I had seen the children inside the host again, he smiled. He did not doubt that this was happening for me. He understood that God will give favors and spiritual consolations as he wills. Oddly, that brought me no consolation. Father must have seen the fear in my face as he said, "Teresa, enjoy this time and accept it as a gift from Our Lord." Father's comment gave me courage to be open to this incredible mystery.

It was a blessing that I was able to speak with Father that afternoon. He could have been out at an appointment, but he was still in the rectory when I got there. Father Josiah believed in the power of the Eucharist - the power of grace and the mercy of God. I needed his approval, his reassurance, to help me to receive this gift of seeing my children. Once again, God provided his priest to guide me.

For the next several weeks during Lent everyday, I would see my children inside the host at our Eucharistic adoration chapel. The encouragement from my husband and Father Josiah continued to provide the support that I needed to relax during these holy hours and embrace this gift from God. This would be the time that Our Lord would show me how to become a mother to my children. I would experience, in a way that is difficult to put into words, a deep intimacy with each of them. While looking at my children inside Our Eucharistic Lord, I began, through grace, to receive this inner knowledge about their personalities. They became three distinct individuals to me. I was learning about them and responding with my heart as though nothing could separate us.

Seeing my children inside the host was beyond incredible. Receiving their names, then seeing their faces, and learning about their characters made them so real to me. I longed to hold them and hug them. As that yearning grew, so did my sorrow. Feeling tremendous guilt about desiring more than I had already been given, I called to my Blessed Mother again. I stood before her unashamed with an open heart. She is my mother, I felt safe with her and confident that I could speak with her about anything. I believed that she understood this desire which I felt to touch my children and to be touched by them. She knew the desires of my heart as a mother and my love for Our Lord. She also knew that I did not want to offend him by asking for more. So I decided to confide in her this daily sorrow that once again I felt. I relied upon her to help me through these emotions that continued to stir within my heart. She is my mother and I can tell her anything, so I held nothing back.

Then one afternoon during Lent at daily mass, I begged Our Lady to help remove this desire to hug my children. I felt afraid of offending God in all the goodness that he showed me. I had just finished my prayer to her when I went up to receive Holy Communion. I returned to my pew and was in deep mediation. I was thinking about my children. Then, in a way that is very difficult to describe, this intense longing that I felt to hold my children was being communicated to Our Lady without any words. At that very moment, I heard the sound of children's footsteps running up the main aisle of the church. Not wanting to be distracted from my meditation by these children in the church, I kept my head down thinking their mother would be running after them in a moment and get them to sit back down. To my great surprise, I then felt two arms grab my waist from behind, immediately I thought Michelle Marie, another two arms embraced my neck, instinctively, I knew it was Daniel John, and yet another two arms clung to my arm, my son, Ezekiel James. I thought, "My children, how is this possible?" I kept my eyes closed and relished in their touch. It was not necessary for me to turn to see them as I knew each child by the way they touched me.

It reminded me of when I gave birth to my two living children. When the nurses in the hospital would wheel the babies to their mother's rooms from the nursery for feeding, you could hear all the babies crying together in the hallway. They were hungry! I knew my baby without seeing my child from the other babies simply by their cry in the hallway. I have spoken to many other mothers about this hospital experience, and they too knew their child by its cry. It is a mother's heart. I realized that this is what the Lord was forming in me - a mother's heart for my three children.

At the end of mass, I waited in the hallway as Father Josiah had been the celebrant. I believe that he could see by the look on my face that something serious had happened to me. I told him what had just occurred during communion. Again, I felt the need for his assurance that this was of God. Father was so happy for me and marveled at the spiritual consolations which I was receiving. It amazed me that God was so gracious to allow Father Josiah to be there that day as the celebrant. Father's reaction would once again assist me in entering into this mystery.

That Easter Sunday in 1998 was the last time I would see my children. This happened during mass while kneeling in meditation after receiving Holy Communion when I longed again to embrace my children for me to be able to touch them, hold them, and hug them. Again, my desire overrode all my sense of rationality. It was hard for me to understand why this yearning was so irresistible and kept surfacing. I could not escape it. As I knelt during that time of communion with Our Lord, I asked his mercy upon me for wanting more, and I asked Our Lady to help to plead with her son for me. While praying, I felt so close to Our Lord and Our Lady in deep meditation with them. Suddenly, my surroundings receded into the background and I felt my daughter, Michelle Marie, in my arms. In my mind's eye, I could clearly see us together. She looked to be about 8 years old. I was leaning down holding her in my embrace; she threw her head back to look up at me. As I buried my face in her long light brown hair, I breathe in its sweet scent as she said, "Mommy." I felt the softness of her cheek as I showered her with kisses. She giggled as she gently held onto my neck. Next, I was standing in front of my son, Ezekiel James. He is taller than me and appeared to be the age of 22. I put my arms around him and nestled my head upon his chest. After awhile, I looked up and softly touched his cheek. He said, "Mother I love you." Lastly, my son, Daniel John, was before me small in stature and he seemed to be age 4. I knelt down and gently embraced him. How round and soft his face was as I ran my fingers around his cheeks! I brushed his dark hair to the side with my hand and held him close to my heart. He said, "Mommy," as I kissed him. It amazed me how all my senses were alive. How real this all felt! It was as though we were allowed to be in our own time and place together for that moment. What an incredible grace!

After these occurrences stopped on that Easter Day, I no longer felt that level of yearning to touch my children or see them. I felt deeply satisfied and content. My desire for heaven increased as I thought about how we would one day be together for all eternity. I still talk to them when I am in the presence of Our Eucharistic Lord. I know that they are praying for me. My motherhood feels natural with them as it has been restored.

Insights I received through the power of the Eucharist:

Through these incredible spiritual favors from God, I received the understanding that reclaiming and restoring my motherhood to my children was the answer to the healing of my wounds from abortion. It was God's generous love and grace which gave me the courage to embrace my motherhood as a present identity. I realized that he used many priests as his vessels to bring me to that place of dignity. It was through their words, their priestly power, their encouragement, and their fatherly guidance that led me to Our Eucharistic Lord where I finally received total peace.

The majestic power of these Eucharistic experiences was not easy for me to receive. As amazing as these spiritual moments are, their power and grace are overwhelming. I quickly learned that I needed the support and guidance from a priest to remain open and receptive to them.

Through the outpouring of grace, I was given a profound understanding about the mystery of the communion of saints, eternal life, and the true presence of Our Lord in the Eucharist. I also discovered that God will heal the old memories of wounds through giving new ones of hope, love, and mercy.

IMPORTANCE OF RESTORED PARENTHOOD

"The Lord is close to the brokenhearted; and those who are crushed in spirit he saves. The Lord redeems the lives of his servants; no one incurs guilt who takes refuge in him".

Psalm 34

Restored motherhood was essential to my healing from the horrific effects of abortion. It was through the gift of receiving my children's names and learning about them through our Eucharistic Lord that led me on the path to discover that I was being called to reclaim my present position of motherhood. Each occurrence was bringing me closer to that place.

Through the post-abortive healing programs, I had claimed my aborted babies as my children, especially during the retreat that I attended, but I had not embraced my identity as their mother. How could I? I had never formed a bond with them. My only act of parental responsibility toward my children was the choice to destroy them. I had no idea of how such a thing would ever be possible, yet as you have read, with God, nothing is impossible.

It was the Lord who had given me that desire in my heart which was to know my aborted children. I had also been given the grace to trust him and to respond to his promptings which led me into that reunion and restoration. Through the aftermath of such a horrible sin, as you read, God showed me how to rise up into the dignity of my motherhood to my aborted children. This reclaiming was a vital key which unlocked the door of the heart to release the guilt and shame.

I've prayed and thought a lot about the truth of reclaiming parenthood, as I prepared to write to you. How do I translate to you why it was so critical? Through God's grace, it occurred to me to begin by explaining to you what I read about the definition of the word healing. What is healing?

According to Webster's Dictionary, healing is to restore and get rid of the affliction. Once again, according to Webster, the word, restore, means to give back, to return or to put back again into a former or original state. Reunite is to bring together after separation.

This form of spiritual healing, restoration, and reuniting was the way which the Lord led me with assistance of his mother out of the darkness of this sin of abortion. Even though I had accepted that I was forgiven by God and my children, even though I released gut-wrenching sorrow and believed that they were in heaven with him, I had not experienced restoration or had felt reunited with my children. Instead, as you read, I had felt constant longing for them and the pain of that separation. I never understood how important it was for me to focus on my position as their mother in addition to accepting the fact that they are my children. No one had brought this to my attention or discussed this aspect with me aside from Father Josiah when he said, "You are as much a mother today to those children as the day you aborted them." It was that moment of grace with Father Josiah that pointed me in this direction. Did Father Josiah realize the weight of his words when he said "You are as much a mother today to your children as the day you aborted them?" I believe so. When I approached Father with all these spiritual consolations and favors granted me with my children that took place before our Eucharistic Lord, he was well aware that God was restoring me. Who would know better the power of grace and the mercy of God than a priest?

I realized that I had not only aborted my children but also had abandoned my position as their mother. Both aspects of this parent- child relationship had to be addressed for me to experience complete healing. I learned when Our Lord heals, it means that he restores, not replaces. I had to be put back into my original position, not into the position of remembering my children as people of the past, instead of eternal souls. Therefore, I had to be restored to relationship with my children. My dignity would come through embracing my current position and title as mother to my aborted children.

The parable of the prodigal son is an excellent story that illustrates such restoration to dignity. Upon reading and meditating on this story, I began to parallel this parable of the Prodigal Son to my story of lost motherhood through sin.

I imagined myself in this story as a Prodigal daughter. A post-abortive person, who squandered the treasures I was given, aborting my children, gifts given by God. After I committed such grievous acts against God and my children, could it be possible for me to be restored back to my original position as a mother to them like the young man who was restored back to the position of son?

Once there was genuine repentance on my part over my decision of abortion, "Father I have sinned against you and my children. Michelle Marie, Ezekiel James, and Daniel John, forgive me for aborting you," would the Father restore my position as mother or kiss me and leave me with my intense desire to be a mother again to them. Had I lost the essence of my motherhood forever? Would the Father say to me, "You can come in my child, and I will help you start again, but that title of mother is all you receive and it is a memory until you get to heaven one day." Is that how the Father will respond to my repentance? Did the father in the story say to the son, you will always be known as my son, but you cannot regain the full essence of that position or relationship? Trust was broken between us, so the intimacy of a father-son relationship will take time to eventually be restored.

When the Prodigal son returned to his father, it was not only forgiveness that the son received but also full restoration to his position as son. The father immediately put sandals on his feet, which signified that he was not a servant any longer, rather, his son. His father then put the robe on him and family ring which signified that he resumed his position in the family as son. And so, the story goes on about the celebration, because he not only was forgiven but also was restored to where he always belonged in his father's eyes as his beloved son, part of the family with all its entitlements and privileges.

The father in the story shows us the true mercy of God when the father immediately gives his child back all the dignity as his son. All at once, the position that the son held before he left and committed such grievous acts is reinstated. The father does this through his kiss, placing the robe, sandals, ring upon his son and calling for a celebration. This is done not only just for his son's sake but also for the whole town to recognize his son as his child with all the distinction it brings. What was lost had been restored fully all at once. That is how great the Father's mercy is for us too who genuinely repent to him.

After reflecting on this parable, I realized even more deeply the truth God wanted me to understand. It wasn't enough for me to repent, to remember, and to memorialize my children as people of the past as though they are not eternal living souls. I needed to accept my position as their mother as my true place. God never stopped seeing me as their mother. I moved away from that position out of my sense of unworthiness. Through reestablishing my title and position as their mother, I was fully accepting his mercy and love. I know that it was only through his grace that this was possible. To not receive this would have been like the prodigal son saying to his father that I will come home, but father, I must remain your servant to be given no more. He would accept his father's mercy and forgiveness, but he couldn't experience the fruit of the father's immense mercy unless he stepped back into his position of son by accepting the ring, sandals, and fine robe.

John Paul II says in the Gospel of Life to those who aborted children, "understand what happened and face it honestly. If you have not already done so, give yourselves over with humility and trust to repentance. The Father of mercies is ready to give you his forgiveness and his peace in the Sacrament of Reconciliation. You will come to understand that nothing is definitively lost."

Through grace, I experienced that understanding about nothing being definitively lost that the Holy Father speaks of in this document. Our Father's mercy is immense. He in his own mystical and divine way led me to total restoration - not to only be forgiven as his child but also to be given back the dignity of my motherhood. It is as though he said to me, "Come Teresa, let me welcome you back, and put your children back into your arms. Let me teach you about your children and nurture your love for one another." How tremendous is that love and mercy! How amazing is that reality! Something that I never imagined possible became a present title.

However, this experience of receiving mercy after committing such a grievous sin takes support, encouragement, and tremendous grace. God knew that I could not do this alone. I needed help. My support came through the priests and the seminarian in my story.

You read about Frank, the seminarian, who introduced me to the truths about our Blessed Mother. His encouragement put me on the path of developing a relationship with her. Then, Father Raymond to whom I confessed my abortions gave me the penance to listen to "Be not Afraid." He wanted to encourage me to follow Jesus and believe the Lord would give me peace. Father Tim understood the power of grace when I told him that I saw my children for the first time at the gate with Jesus. Father Tim helped me to recognize the reason this was revealed to me. He taught me about reparation for sin, especially regarding my abortions. Father Pedro recognized that I had unrepented sin and encouraged general confession. He knew that I needed to feel deeper contrition for my sin. Father Bernard, the priest from the retreat, encouraged me to believe in the power and mystery of the Eucharistic through his words, "When you are in the presence of Jesus they will be there too." Father Josiah set me on the path to recognizing that my motherhood was not lost to my aborted children when he said, "You are as much a mother today to your children as the day you aborted them."

Do you see how important these priests were in the journey of my post-abortive healing? It was their words, their priestly power in the sacraments, and their fatherly guidance that not only led me to Our Eucharistic Lord but also helped me to remain before him in the mystery of his grace where I finally received total peace. There is no replacement for his priests. Who else could have understood the movement of the spirit, the power of grace, and the condition of the soul? It is you who are the divine physicians through the reception of that unique sacramental grace bestowed upon you when ordained into the vocation of priesthood. You were a vital part of my post-abortive healing.

CONCLUSION

I realize the spiritual consolations, favors, insights, and certitude that I received came through an out pouring of grace in an extraordinary way. Therefore, I was given the means to accept and understand them. In 1998, when my spiritual director at the time, Father Josiah told me to write down my story, he also warned me about it. He said, "When you share your story, not everyone will have the grace to receive what you say." All these years, his words have remained with me. For this reason, I have prayed for you since 2011 that you will have the grace to receive whatever Our Lord wants to show you through my story.

In conclusion, I would like to now share with you a few approaches that I have learned when meeting with men and women who have aborted their children. On numerous occasions, I have had the privilege to pray with post-abortive parents. Through my healing experience, I understand the importance of Our Lady as a journey mate. Therefore, before conversation begins, I pray with the parent. I call upon the Blessed Mother, asking that she hold us under her mantle and give us every grace according to our needs. I remind her that she understands well the sorrowful heart of a parent. Then, I say the Memorare slowly and meaningfully, so the parent can hear that "never was it known" that Our Lady has not helped those who turn to her. Next, I pray to their aborted children by name if they have one, if not, I say child/children of ... please pray with Our Lady before Our Lord for your Mom/Dad right now.

The result was quite powerful. Post-abortive parents have shared with me that when they heard their son or daughter called upon by name to pray for them, their fear lessened. They expressed a feeling of incredible peace and a greater receptivity to the Holy Spirit. Their joy increased and they felt comforted. They were, in essence, experiencing their present position as parents to their aborted child in that moment of prayer.

Secondly, because I received such a certainty about the importance of restored parenthood, I began to speak with others about this idea when they would share their sorrow with me over their unborn children. I was given the confidence through grace to believe that this type of spiritual healing was not for me alone. I felt secure in encouraging others to go before Our Eucharistic Lord through the assistance of Our Lady for healing. I would say, "Talk to her. She is your Mother; tell her all your heart feels. She will understand. Then ask Our Lady to help you with this sorrow and to bring you closer to your aborted child. Do this when you are in the presence of our Eucharistic Lord." I did not assure the person that anything will definitively happen, although I believed it would, I merely suggested it.

The most astonishing things occurred when others did this and experienced the power of Our Eucharistic Lord. Each time, I received an email or phone call of excitement from that parent with the news of an astounding spiritual favor from Our Lord to help them know their aborted child. Needless to say, these parents were elated and transitioned out of that deep sorrow into the joy and dignity of their parenthood.

Although I cannot share the details of these amazing stories as they are sacred and private experiences meant only to be shared by their parents, I can tell you this; each post- abortive parent received exactly what they needed from Our Lord. Incredible spiritual consolations would occur for each of them, such as seeing their aborted child, hearing their aborted child's voice speaking to them, or discovering the gender of their aborted child. He gave them a new memory when they thought of their child. Each parent was given exactly what they needed for restoration, receiving just what they desired - no more, no less. Our Eucharistic Lord gave each person what was necessary to increase their dignity as a parent and to receive his mercy.

Having experienced the power of the Eucharist, the vast mercy and love of God, the faithfulness of Our Lady, and her intercession, has placed within me a depth of understanding and surety about the importance of restored parenthood for post-abortive parents. How is it possible that God would bestow such spiritual favors upon these wounded parents? It is a mystery which I accept and believe firmly. I have experienced it and witnessed it in others that with God, all things are possible.

I pray that what I have shared with you will be of some assistance. I am forever grateful to every priest who was part of my post-abortive healing journey. Without their comments, reactions, whether positive or negative, and their guidance as well administering the sacraments, I believe that I would not have reached the depth of healing which I received. In every instance, it was their words and actions above all others that affected me. There is no replacement for the priest who holds the power of Christ within his vocation.

I encourage you to trust the gift you hold for those suffering. They are caught between sorrow and distress. You know the way out of that is through Our Lord. You, in Persona Christi are the divine healer, the physician of the soul. Believe in the power of Our Eucharistic Lord and trust the priestly power given to you. Have confidence in him who works through your humanness by the grace of your vocation. It is you who help us to become disposed to the graces you know that we can receive. Remember, it is only you who calls him from heaven to be present with us in the Eucharist where miracles occur. *I am forever…In Gratitude… to you.*

ABOUT THE AUTHOR

Teresa Lanowich lives in South Florida with her husband of 38 years. She is a certified Spiritual Director and directs Marian themed retreats for women. Teresa is also a facilitator for a married couples' ministry in which various discussion series on the church's teachings about marriage and family life are offered.

Teresa would be honored to come and speak to priests about her post abortive healing. For scheduling a talk or any other inquiries contact her at InHisMercy5@gmail.com